For Roger
and all our rainy days to come –
with all my love,
Robin
January 8, 1972

Rain Rain Rivers

To Isabel Wright

Rain Rain Rivers

Words and Pictures by Uri Shulevitz

Farrar, Straus and Giroux / New York

It is raining outside.
I can hear it.

The rain is pattering on the window.

The rain is pattering on the roof.

It rains all over town.

Rain rolls down the roofs,
rushing down the eaves,
gushing out the drainpipes.

Streams stream in the gutters.

Tomorrow I'll sail my little boats.

It rains!
It rains over fields.

It rains over hills.

It rains over grass.

It rains over ponds too.

Frogs,
stop your croaking!
Take cover in the water
and listen to the rain.

It pours.

Streams are streaming.

Rills roll down hills,
fall into brooks,
rush into rivers and race to the seas.

Waves billow and roll,
Rush, splash and surge,
Rage, roar and rise.

Oceans are swelling,
Melting the skies.

It rains.
Tomorrow new plants will grow.

Birds will bathe in the streets.

We'll run barefoot in puddles and stamp in warm mud.

I'll jump over pieces of sky in the gutter.

It rains all over town.
The plant on my window
is beginning to grow.
I know it.